Ama

Amazon Echo For Beginners

A Simple User Guide To Learn Amazon Echo Now

Table Of Contents

Introduction

Are you the type of person who keeps forgetting appointments? Ever want to blast music that's loud and clear at home? Have you ever wanted a device that you could connect with other devices at home?

Well, maybe it's time for you to try Amazon Echo!

Considered as a voice recognition device slash speaker, Amazon Echo, also known as Alexa, provides hands-free voice control, that's in this midrange bass and well-balanced treble range.

Ever since its incarnation in November 2014, Amazon Echo has taken the world by storm. In short, it can make life a whole lot easier because it reminds you of your appointments and other important events; helps you stream music from various websites and apps, and allows you to make use of tricks and even Easter Eggs to make the experience of using Alexa all the more worthwhile!

With the help of this guide, you'll be introduced to Alexa, get to know how she can help you out, and understand how you can personalize the use of the said device.

Surely, after reading this book, using Alexa would no longer be a problem. Read this book now to find out how.

Let's begin the journey.

Chapter 1: Amazon Echo and Alexa

So, first and foremost: Who is Alexa?

Alexa is a cloud service that works with Amazon Echo as a voice recognition service. If Echo is the device, Alexa serves as the mind—and this is why you get the right kind of information that you are looking for.

Features

What exactly can you expect from Amazon Echo? How does it look and feel like?

Well, for starters, it comes in the color black, with the dimensions 9.25 x 3.27 inches, with 1 subwoofer that comes in 2.5 inches.

It has 2 inch tweeters, and makes use of adapter power, and could be bought for $199!

Homescreen

Take note that the homescreen on your Echo app is basically a support system that shows you your most recent interaction with the device. There are home screen cards that you can tap so you can see user-specific controls.

You can check out Alexa's homescreen on the Alexa App (more on this later). This means you'll be able to see the following:

1. **Home.** This is the homepage of the device that displays recordings and activities.

2. **Alarm.** This is where you'd set the alarm for the next day, or for other important events and reminders.

3. **Timer.** This shows whether the timer has been turned on or off. This also allows you to put the timer on pause.

4. **List.** This is where you'd see shopping and to-do lists.

5. **Music Provider.** This will show you the device's music library.

From Project D to Echo

During its development stage, it was called Project D, which stands for Doppler that took around four years to finally come into place. The wait's worth it, though, because Alexa is able to do a lot of things. Actually, there are some essential things that you have to know about it—and these are:

It is a Bluetooth speaker

Being a Bluetooth speaker, it means you can stream music from your iPhone6, and you'd be able to experience such a clear quality of sounds, thanks to Alexa's advanced audio design found in a cylindrical chassis inside the microphone.

You see, when you open up Alexa, you'll see that there are speakers that are considered as dual-downward firing that are able to transmit sound all around the room—in 360 degrees!

Apart from that, you'll also find that Alexa has a 2 inch tweeter that provides high and low differences in sound, as well as a 2.5 inch woofer reflex port that helps provide clearer, deeper sounds without any form of distortion. More so, Alexa comes with music playback controls and a built-in mic.

It is said to be the predecessor of the "Internet Home"

The Internet Home stems from the belief about the "Internet of Things", which means that one day, every single thing you have at home might be connected to each other for easy functionality!

Since the Amazon Echo will be able to answer your questions and help you out with a lot of things, you can expect that one day, it might be developed into something even better—which would then be able to adapt to the ever-changing world that we're all living in.

It could be used with the Amazon Pen

Recent developments made Amazon release the pen. This is a device that can be paired with Alexa but its main function is to record conversations while you are outside the house. This means you can write ideas literally on paper while the pen is playing what you have previously recorded. Pretty much, this is a recording tool designed as a pen which has a capacity of 4GB of data storage. 4GB is close to storing about 400 hours of talk time. It does not come with the package and has to be purchased separately.

It always listens

You see, one of the main things about Alexa is that she can access streaming services—even without a display setting saying that it is now trying to access the said services.

This happens because Alexa has a seven-microphone array that works like a far-field voice recognition service, which literally means that it's always on—and it's always listening, and it works because of a beam-forming technology that is unique to the Amazon Echo. This also helps Alexa cancel the noise around you so you could just concentrate on the music—or whatever it is that you're trying to stream.

The search function is so easy to use

Alexa is basically the cloud streaming service that serves as search function for the Amazon Echo. This is why every time you need to ask it something, you have to say the word "Alexa" first. It's like getting someone's attention: You have to make sure that you know this person, and that you know his name—it's like you're giving Alexa some respect, too, which she really deserves because she'll be able to help you out with a lot of things!

The Alexa App

You know, one great thing about Alexa is that its functionality does not end on the speaker, mic, and remote alone. It actually comes with an app that's meant for Amazon Fire Phones, as well as Android Handsets, and it is also believed that more apps might be created in time, as the device progresses.

The app can be used to help you do whatever you are doing better. While Alexa could work on its own, it is also good to feel like you have some extra help when you need it.

You could also use the Remote Control

The remote control is a back-up command system. It is five inches in length and designed with a rubberized grip to prevent it from slipping from your hands. To activate the remote control, you need to turn it on by pushing the button found on top of the Amazon Echo device. Once turned on, you can speak to the remote control at farther distances.

The remote will transmit your message to the main device and Alexa will process your command. The remote control comes with a magnetic holster to allow you to take it anywhere in the house without having to carry it by hand. You can hook it to your belt and attached the remote, thereby giving you mobility with the remote control.

Chapter 2: Set Up and Use

In order to use Amazon Echo, of course, it's just imperative that you learn how to set it up first.

Set-Up

To do this, you first have to download the Alexa App on your phone. You could find this on *http://alexa.amazon.com/* and make sure that you are using the following platforms:

1. iOS tablets or phones in iOS 7.0 (Apple)

2. Android 4.0 and above (Android/Google)

3. Fire 2.0 and above (Fire tablets/phones)

Then, go ahead and plug the device to an outlet and prepare the remote control by inserting the batteries that came along with it. Once the remote is turned on, it will automatically pair itself with the device. If the remote does not pair, do this: Go to the Echo App in your mobile device then go to *Settings > Amazon Echo > Pair Remote/Forget Remote*. Wait for the devices to pair. If it is unsuccessful, you need to contact Amazon support.

If it is successfully paired, it is time to give your device a name. To do this, go back to your app *Settings* and select *Your Amazon Echo*. Delete this and type the name you want your device to be called. Tap on *Save Changes*. This name has no impact on the wake word of the device, which is still *Alexa* or *Amazon*. The purpose of the name is to simply personalize the device. You may have more than one Amazon Echo in your home and this lets you know which one has been paired to which device or not.

It's also important that you connect the device to the Wi-Fi. The Echo was designed to work only in dual band Wi-Fi. This means that it cannot work on enterprise or corporate type of Wi-Fi connections.

Press and hold the Action button on the device for five seconds. Wait until you see the light turn orange; this is an indication that the device is connecting to your Wi-Fi. Next, go to *Settings > ECHO > Update Wi-Fi*. You should see a list of available Wi-Fi connections. Select yours then tap *Connect*.

If you cannot locate your Wi-Fi from the list, scroll down to the bottom and select *Add a Network Rescan*. The device will scan the environment again for available connections. If this still fails, you need to set-up your Amazon Echo device close to the router so it can pick up signals. Signals are usually blocked by walls. Moving your Amazon Echo main unit closer to the router should eliminate issues like this.

Using the Echo

Now, you have to start testing the device. Of course, it all starts with its Wake Word.

The ring on top of the device should turn white—an indication that your Echo is ready and that it is already connected to the Amazon Cloud or server. The next thing to do is to test if it can hear you. Change the default settings to ensure that it is programmed accordingly. Go the Echo App on your mobile device and select *Settings> [your Echo Name] > Sounds > set Wake Up Sound to Enabled*. Now, test the device. Say the wake word, which is either "Alexa" or "Amazon", and listen closely if you hear a soft beep. It indicates that the device is fully set up.

Amazon Echo, just like other Voice Recognition products, uses a certain mechanism called *on-device keyword spotting* which helps it detect the Wake Word, and also allows it to stream audio to the Cloud, and then there's a certain audio sample that's also sent to the Cloud to help understand what you're trying to say.

However, if there is one family member who is named Alexa, you can change the device's wake up word to Amazon. To do this, go to *Settings > Wake Word > Amazon.*

If you want to make sure that your voice is heard and that the device is connecting you to the Amazon Cloud, go to *Settings > [your Echo name] > Wake Up Sound.* Enable this and the device will produce a beeping sound every time it wakes up in response to your command. You can also program it to produce a sound once it is done uploading your command to the Amazon Cloud. Do this by enabling *End of Request.*

Amazon's voice recognition program is unparalleled. To date, there were very few complaints logged in Amazon and she sounds almost human, far less robotic than iPhone's SIRI. According to users, the Amazon Echo has less likelihood of misunderstanding your commands than other voice recognition programs. What Amazon does is to record your voice and consistently improve its comprehension and results. And this is something you can do and improve as you go along the voice training program with Alexa.

Chapter 3: The Different Ring Colors

Another thing you have to understand about the Echo is that various ring colors signify different things about Amazon Echo. Here's what you need to know about them:

Solid Blue

If the color of the ring on top of the device is solid blue, it means that the device is alive—it's awake—and is actually waiting for your commands!

Solid White

If you see solid white, it means that the volume of Amazon Echo is currently being adjusted. For this, you can make use of voice commands, the remote, or the device itself.

Spinning Blue

This means that the device is either processing or booting up. You'll also notice that the direction of the light will be coming to your direction, and it'll only change direction when you move because it will follow the direction of your voice.

Violet

This color means that the Echo is not able to connect to the Wi-Fi in any way. It's also best that you check the device's signal strength when you get to see this color. You could also try rebooting the modem or the device itself.

Solid Red

Solid Red Light means that the Echo's microphone has been turned off, and that your commands would not be heard—and you also wouldn't get any answers from the device.

No Color

And, if the ring doesn't show any color, it means that even though the device has been turned on, it is still waiting for you to say the wake word. This is because Amazon Echo has been naturally designed to go on "Snooze" mode when it is not being used.

To turn the microphone off, you should push the microphone button on top of the Echo. When you see that it's red, it means you have turned the microphone off, and that it would not respond to your Wake Word. However, it would still respond to your commands as long as you have the Amazon Echo Remote.

Chapter 4: How Amazon Echo Can Help You

Start Voice Training Alexa

In order to use Alexa the way you want to, you have to make sure that you start training her. You can then follow the Voice Training Exercise below to help Alexa gain skills.

As you progress in the voice training, the device will record your voice multiple times and will help it understand you better. It will record the many ways you say a word and officially recognize that it is you. Alexa will match your speech patterns better and will produce results for you faster and more accurately.

To start voice training, make sure the microphone is turned on by pressing the button on top of the device. Do not use the remote during voice training. Your intent is to record your voice clearly and allow Alexa to process this. Next time you speak to it, even in a muffled voice, Alexa should be able to recognize you. The voice training results will also help the device recognize what you say over the remote control's microphone.

Next, launch your Echo app from your phone, select *Voice Training > Start*.

The system will ask you to read 25 different phrases. Ideally, you should speak from a distance where you will be barking your commands most of the time. You should speak clearly and normally. Do not attempt to toy with the speed or clarity of your speech because the system will record this as a standard reference. Talk to it as you normally would. No need to be self-conscious here. It is a device, not a person who will ridicule you.

If you think you need to repeat a word, tap on Pause in the app and select *Repeat Phrase*. Once done, tap on *Next Phrase* and move on to the succeeding phases. This process can take a while. If you feel tired, you can tap on *Pause* and *End Session* then continue when you feel comfortable.

Even if you skip the exercise, Alexa will still record all the phrases you read and upload it to the Amazon Cloud. You can continue at a later time until you are completely done with the voice training exercise. In addition, the things you say in the voice training exercise will not be recorded in your dialogue box or panel so it will not be crowded.

Speaking of skills, you need to keep in mind that these are basically Alexa's voice-driven capabilities. You can actually tweak those skills by enabling or disabling them. Doing so is called *invocation*. You can do this after activating Alexa, of course.

The thing with skills is that when you make use of specific phrases (i.e., *Turn TV On, Abracadabra Radio*, etc.), you somehow get to communicate with the developer of the original skill. Prime examples would be asking for zip codes, asking Alexa to tell some trivia, or even those Easter Egg commands. As the world progresses, it's important to help the developers work on the app to make them applicable to the world you're living in. Plus, when you help developers enhance Alexa's skills, those skills in turn would contain more information.

Using Bluetooth

Next, you have to be able to control it with the help of Bluetooth technology. This is mainly because if you want to experience a pure and clear musical adventure, you should know how to work the Echo through its Bluetooth feature.

With Echo, you do not have to manipulate the recording via your phone. Alexa is equipped with the capability to control playback on your device. All you need to do is to sync her to your device and pick the track you want to play by using voice commands:

1. Play

2. Previous

3. Pause

4. Next

5. Stop

6. Restart

Turn on your phone's Bluetooth and set your phone closely to the Amazon Echo main unit then say, "Alexa, pair." This will prompt Alexa to look for a Bluetooth connection. Once she finds your device she will say, "Ready to pair." Now go to your phone and select Alexa and pair. Once successful, Alexa will tell you, "Connected to Bluetooth." Your mobile handset will also give you the usual Bluetooth confirmation.

Now, you can stream all the songs you want directly from your mobile device. Alexa will play these songs if you use the Echo app or the remote if you do not want to give a voice command. Once you are finished, you can tell Alexa to disconnect. Take note that you cannot send and receive photos and videos using Alexa's Bluetooth technology. Her software does not allow her to do this because she is only a speaker.

Once a Bluetooth device has been paired, Alexa will remember it. You do not have to manually pair it again. As long as your mobile device's Bluetooth is on, you can tell Alexa to pair and she will do it automatically.

Managing the Remote

The remote control allows you to give Alexa commands if you are farther than the usual range covered by the device. The remote control has a microphone that allows it to hear you. Once you have given a command, the remote control will relay the signal to the device, then the device will start working on the task you want it to get done.

To tune on the remote, push the button on top of the remote until you hear a beeping sound. Continue holding it down while you are giving it instructions. The remote control does not have a wake word and does not require one. The remote will also allow you to give orders to Alexa even if the device's microphones are muted. Sometimes, you need to mute the device's microphones if there is too much noise or chatter in the room. The alternative is to use the remote to give it orders.

In Chapter 1, we mentioned that the remote has to be paired with the device. If you lost the remote or if it is damaged, you may order a replacement but you have to pair it again. To do this, go to *Settings > [your Echo name] > Pair Remote/Forgot Remote> Forget*. This command will tell the device to forget the old remote control. Then pair the new remote control.

The remote is also equipped with buttons that allow you to adjust the volumes and, stop, and pause what is blaring through the device. You can use these controls if you do not want to talk to Alexa—times when you are having a conversation with someone and you do not want to be rude.

Review what you have told Alexa

You could also review the commands you've been telling Alexa.

All you have to do is access the Alexa app then go to Settings, and choose History. Take note that you'll then see a compilation of commands that you have categorized into *requests* and *questions*.

To see more detailed entries, all you have to do is tap one of those commands, and you'll be provided with details about it, plus you can also listen to the audio, and you can then provide feedback so that in case Alexa wasn't able to answer it right, you can then tell her how exactly she needs to answer it next time.

Also, you have to take note that history may not really show what you have said verbatim, but you can expect that they will pretty much reflect the commands you have used. It's best that you use the review option, though, because it will help improve Alexa by a mile.

Shopping on Amazon

Of course, you could also use Alexa to shop for various products on Amazon.

However, you have to make sure that you're only shopping for legitimate products/brands, and products that are also visible on Prime. Your Amazon account addresses and billing information will be the default settings used so you'd easily be able to place orders.

You can also tweak settings by asking for confirmation code, see product and order details, and even turn purchasing off. Orders placed on Amazon Echo are subject to the same rules that are used for Amazon and Amazon Prime Purchases, as well.

The Amazon Echo is programmed to add items in your things-to-do-list each time you give it the right command. Just say, "Alexa, add beer to my to-do list." The device will add this automatically and in addition, the list in your Echo app will also be updated. You can do this in two ways—you tell Alexa verbally to add something in the list or you can go to your app and navigate the to-do-list from the control panel and update it manually.

Alexa can store up to 100 items per list. That is a lot if you really think about it. You can now forget about cluttered papers around your house and forgotten lists. You can tell Alexa to update the list everytime you remember something and also delete some if you want to.

Basically, Alexa supports shopping lists and to-do-lists. You can create your own shopping list so you have it handy when you go to the grocery store. All you need to do is to check it on your smartphone using the Echo app. In fact, you can tell Alexa to buy this instantly from Amazon and deliver it to you for as long as it is available on Amazon.com.

If you are unsure what is in your shopping list, you can ask, "Alexa, what is on my shopping list?" Alexa will enumerate what is on the list and you can tell her to stop or to delete an item. Example: "Delete beer." To tell her to stop, say, "Alexa, stop" or "Alexa, pause."

You also have to remember that there is a long wait list for this device but if you are lucky enough to be even invited, you can toggle something in your account to make the shipping faster. Go to your account settings and go to *Open Orders*. Click this and you will see the tentative date of shipping for your Amazon Echo. Here, select FREE shipping.

If you have already selected a shipping preference before, click that same preference. Then click on *Confirm*. Do not change your original shipping preference to another one because you will be put back to the end of the queue. All you have to do is to click the current shipping preference again, as if to tell the system that you are desperate to have this device now.

Many Amazon subscribers have reported that this trick works but this is not guaranteed. At best, you just have to be patient or buy a second-hand Amazon Echo from online marketplaces.

If you don't want to use Alexa for purchasing and don't want others to use the device for that purpose, too, just visit the Alexa App, go to Settings, and then choose Voice Purchasing, and turn it off.

Chapter 5: Music Commands

You have to remember that Amazon Echo was primarily designed to work with Prime, also known as Amazon's very own music streaming service.

This means that you could get access to *iTunes, Pandora, iHeartRadio, TuneIn,* and *Spotify*—just some of the world's most recognized streaming services, which means that you'd really get the best listening experience!

This is a great move for Amazon because their consumers will not feel boxed in a single music platform. There was a time when Apple did this. Almost all their contents—from books to music— were exclusively bought from iTunes. Although this irked many Apple consumers, this did not reduce Apple's fan base because of its constant innovation.

To ensure that you enjoy this feature, you need to consistently update the version of your Amazon Echo app. If you do not do this, your Echo may not work appropriately and failure to update the app can cause very serious problems later on that may force you to completely re-set up the device.

From time to time, Amazon will add extra developments to their products so be on the lookout if there is something new. It is possible that your Echo will not sync so make sure that you are always updated. In addition, you may need new phones that can support upgraded applications. Sometimes, though, you only need to update your existing phone's firmware.

If you are unsure, go to the store of your device's supported platform—Google Play for Android, iTunes for Apple. Look for Amazon Echo. If there is an update button in the store, tap that. If there is none, your device has the most updated version. Your

Echo app will also automatically update if there is an existing one, provided you are online. If you set up your phone to ask you first before updating, the Echo app will do just that.

Once you have registered your Echo app, it automatically syncs your Amazon Prime library. This can take some time to complete, especially if you have thousands of songs. If you do not have this set up yet, you'd better be a member so you can enjoy millions of free music. In addition, you can upgrade your account to upload 250, 000 songs to your computer! Even if you don't, you will still get to enjoy a lot of music for free if you are subscribed to Amazon Radio. What's more, if you are registered on Amazon Radio you can tell Alexa to directly purchase the song that you just heard and add it to your library so you can listen to it again and again.

Now, since Alexa is already synced to your Amazon Prime account, you just need to tell her to play a specific song. Say, "Alexa, play [song title].' Alexa will scan your library and play that song right away. If there are two songs of the same title, Alexa will tell you that and you just have to select which artist or album you want her to play.

If the song is not in your library, Alexa will surf Amazon to check if it is available. An alternative to this is using the Echo app from your mobile device. You can open your library from there and pick the specific song you want to play. But this takes out the fun because you want to enjoy the voice recognition intelligence of Alexa. Maybe you should only do this if you are talking to somebody so as not to be disrespectful.

To play music from other libraries, you need to sync them to Echo. Go to *Settings > Music Services* then select your library—iTunes, TuneIN, etc... Once it is full synced, the app will get a list of the songs from your 3rd party music application and relay this to Alexa. You need to say the same command. Only this time, Alexa will not surf your Amazon Prime library. Instead, it will surf your iTunes.

You can tell Alexa to like or dislike a song. You can tell her "thumbs up" or "thumbs down" and she will update your preferences. If you noticed that she is playing the same track once in a while, you can say, "I am tired of this song." What she'll do is to remove this song from your playlist. While playing songs, you can also tell Alexa to stop, pause, or restart. You can also tell her to lop or shuffle or play the next song.

Take note that the device can record everything, even a whisper, if it is turned on. You cannot turn this feature off but you can delete recording from the app. This is a security and privacy concern for many people and this is understandable. Amazon made it a point that an Amazon Echo user has the option to delete what has been recorded.

Go to *Manage my Device* page and you can select the recordings you can delete. It is not generally advised to delete everything because it will have a negative impact on how the device recognizes your voice and commands. If you delete everything, you may have to perform voice exercises again.

Other Important Music Commands to Remember:

Here are some of the best music commands you could use:

1. Alexa, what's playing?
2. Alexa, Volume 4
3. Alexa, thumbs up/ Alexa thumbs down (say these when a song from iHeartRadio or Prime Music is playing)
4. Alexa, stop the music
5. Alexa, softer
6. Alexa, shuffle my R & B playlist

7. Alexa, shuffle my new music

8. Alexa, resume

9. Alexa, play the song I just bought

10. Alexa, play some Prime Music

11. Alexa, play some music by Ariana Grande

12. Alexa, play some music

13. Alexa, play me the album I just bought

14. Alexa, play Lips Are Movin'

15. Alexa, play jazz from iHeartRadio

16. Alexa, play a sad song

17. Alexa, next song
18. Alexa, mute
19. Alexa, loop

20. Alexa, I like this song (Also do this when using Prime. This will add a positive rating to the song you have just played)

21. Alexa, buy this song (for Amazon Music)

22. Alexa, buy this album (for Amazon Music)

23. Alexa, add this song

Chapter 6: The Intelligence of Alexa

So, how else could Amazon Echo help you aside from what was given? Well, there are a variety of other things that it can help you with, and ways that it could make your life better.

Getting Localized Information

See, what's great about Alexa is that it doesn't give you information that you probably wouldn't use—such as the weather on the other side of the coast, or the nearest restaurant in Nice, France, if you're actually from Los Angeles, California.

Anyway, Alexa is still working for US Zones—as of now—so, if you ask Alexa what tomorrow's weather will be immediately after finishing the setup, you might end up disappointed. This is because the Echo needs to correctly get your location before giving out such information.

In order to set this, go back to your settings and enter your zip code on the "Echo device location" option. This will allow you to get the correct news (both local and international), and even pre-recorded shows relative to your area.

Since Echo is configured to use only US zip codes, it cannot read localized information from others.

You may decide to go around this by typing in a US zip code anyway, though the time won't work right. If you use the local time, your setup may also be affected as some countries do not implement daylight saving time (which the Echo is configured to use by default). Either way, you will not be able to access weather, traffic, and news reports that suit your region.

Managing Your To-Do List

Managing one's to-do list could be such a drag and that's why it's good to know that Alexa could help you manage your to-do list—so you could attend to your appointments and do what you have to do without having a hard time!

Take note that the Amazon Echo is programed to add items in your things-to-do-list everytime you give it the right command. Just say, "Alexa, add beer to my to-do list." The device will add this automatically and in addition, the list in your Echo app will also be updated. You can do this in two ways—you tell Alexa verbally to add something in the list or you can go to your app and navigate the to-do-list from the control panel and update it manually.

Alexa can store up to 100 items per list. That is a lot if you really think about it. You can now forget about cluttered papers around your house and forgotten lists. You can tell Alexa to update the list everytime you remember something and also delete some if you want to.

Basically, Alexa supports shopping lists and to-do-lists. You can create your own shopping list so you have it handy when you go to the grocery store. All you need to do is to check it in your smartphone using the Echo app. In fact, you can tell Alexa to buy this instantly from Amazon and deliver it to you for as long as it is available in Amazon.com.

If you are unsure what is in your shopping list, you can ask, "Alexa, what is on my shopping list?" Alexa will enumerate what is on the list and you can tell her to stop or to delete an item. Example: "Delete beer." To tell her to stop, say, "Alexa, stop" or "Alexa, pause."

You could also try the following commands:

1. Alexa, add olive oil to my shopping list.

2. Alexa, create a to-do.

3. Alexa, I need a vet's appointment.

4. Alexa, I need to buy pills.

5. Alexa, I need to go to the country club on Saturday.

6. Alexa, put change tire on my to-do list.

Choosing Brands

Alexa has the capability to give you brand names if you are shopping. You can tell her, "Alexa, what can I buy for my wife?" She will blurt out a list of brand names to choose from. Alexa can also tell you prices at a specific shopping center if you tell her this specifically.

When you want to shop and you are looking for prices within your budget range, you can ask Alexa for some great some deals. The Echo app will display those that are within your budget range. This should help you balance your spending and keep your financial life healthy.

Alarm and Timer

Now, you do not need a separate alarm clock because Alexa can wake you up based on your desired time. Sure enough, you already have an alarm clock in your mobile phone but the speakers of Alexa are better.

You have to command Alexa to wake you up at a specific time by saying, "Alexa, wake me up at 7:30 AM." Alexa will automatically set the alarm. What is good about this is even if you set the device in mute, Alexa will not stop alarming until you tell her to snooze. Once you tell her, "Alexa, snooze," she will stop but will start blaring again after nine minutes. Alexa will not reset the alarm herself. You need to tell her to set the alarm at the same time again.

The timer works in the same fashion. You can tell Alexa the number of hours or minutes before she alarms. From time to time, she will tell you how much time is left on the timer. You also have to tell her to "pause timer" if this is what you want her to do.

For this, you could also use the following commands:

1. Alexa, cancel the alarm.

2. Alexa, set the alarm for 8:30 a.m.

3. Alexa, set the timer for 10 minutes.

4. Alexa, wake me up at 6 in the morning.

5. Alexa, how much time is left on my timer?

6. Alexa, what time is it?

7. Alexa, when's my alarm set for?

8. Alexa, stop. (this is used for timer alarm)

9. Alexa, snooze.

10. Alexa, what's the date?

Restaurant Hunting and Book Shopping

If you are looking for a book, you can tell Alexa to search a specific genre—could be comedy, drama, or horror. Once you ask Alexa, she will give you suitable options that you can choose from and she will also give you a summary.

Remember, you can use the 1-Click buying power if you have decided which book you want to buy.

Alexa can give you a list of the best restaurants in your neighborhood. She can also give you the latest deals or promotions as far as restaurants are concerned. Just tell her, "Alexa, give me restaurant deals."

The News

Alexa will also provide you news if you ask her to. There is a service called Flash Briefing in which Alexa provides the hottest news updates from the Internet. You have the flexibility to customize this as per your requirement by going through the app and setting up your preferences. It is up to you if you want to set up you own categories or use the default. You can choose from the following categories:

1. Business

2. Sports

3. Financial

4. Entertainment

Keep in mind that Amazon will provide news information from preselected news sources only and the information you get may have limitations form city to city.

Sports and Athletics

Alexa is also one big pop culture geek, and a big sports fan, too! Just make sure you have connected certain apps, such as *Pandora, TuneIn,* or *iHeartRadio,* amongst others, to your Amazon Echo account. Try the commands below and see what Alexa will tell you.

1. Alexa, did the Spurs win?
2. Alexa, I need a Foo Fighters Station from Pandora.
3. Alexa, play Fox Sports on iHeartRadio.
4. Alexa, play Kiss FM on TuneIn.
5. Alexa, play NPR.
6. Alexa, play RadioLab.
7. Alexa, what's the score of the LA Lakers game?

Traffic + Weather Information

To get traffic information, first you need to use the Echo app on your phone. You need to set the starting location and your destination. The app, through Alexa, will suggest a route to you. Alexa will also tell you the expected travel time. Some examples of how to ask for traffic are:

1. Alexa, give me an alternate route?

2. Alexa, what is a good commute route?

3. Alexa, what is the expected travel time?

4. Alexa, what is the traffic situation?

To determine the weather, just tell her to tell you the weather and mention a date. Remember, Alexa will only produce the weather forecast for the ZIP code associated with your Amazon account.

Chapter 7: Improving Alexa

Of course, using Alexa doesn't just mean you're just going to take what's being offered and that you wouldn't be thinking of how it can be improved. If you really want to make Alexa yours, why not try the following tips below?

Help her compute

We're not talking about your basic 1+1 -- Alexa can also grasp the concepts of floating decimals, so she can tell you the sum of 3.1416 and 2.24756 in a jiffy.

Allow her to research

While Alexa cannot recite the Prime Directive for you yet, she can tell you that it was also the title of a Star Trek movie. She can also access the Internet to give you direct facts and figures. She can even research how many calories that scoop of ice cream has!

Some sense of Pop Culture

Try asking Alexa to beam you up, or try asking her if she is Skynet, and she will give you hilarious answers. She can respond to a wide variety of pop culture references, as well as a collection of Easter eggs. Keep on experimenting with commands!

Some of these Easter Eggs are as follows:

1. Where in the world is Carmen Sandiego?

2. Where have all the flowers gone?

3. Where do you live?

4. Where do babies come from?

5. Where are you from?

6. Where are my keys? (ask twice)

7. When was (Public Figure) elected/other verb?

8. When is the end of the world?

9. When did (movie) come out?

10. When did (event) happen?

11. When am I going to die?

12. What's in name?

13. What was the Oscar Best Picture in 1996?

14. What was the Lorax?

15. What time is it in (name of city)?

16. What is your quest?

17. What is your favorite color?

18. What is the sound of one hand clapping?

19. What is the meaning of life?

20. What is the loneliest number?

21. What is the distance between (location a) and (location b)?

22. What is the definition of_____?

23. What is the best tablet?

24. What is the airspeed velocity of an unladen swallow?

25. What is love?

26. What does the fox say?

27. What do you think of [Apple/Google/Microsoft]?

28. What color is the dress?

29. What color are your eyes?

30. What are you wearing?

31. What are you going to do today?

32. Warp 10

33. War, what is it good for?

34. Volume 11

35. To be or not to be.

36. These aren't the droids you're looking for.

37. Thank you.

38. Testing 1-2-3

39. Tell me a story.

40. Tea. Earl Grey. Hot.

41. Take me to your leader.

42. Surely you can't be serious.

43. Sing me a song.

44. Simon says Wilford Brimley has diabetes.

45. Show me the money!

46. Set phasers to kill.

47. See you later alligator.

48. Say hello to my little friend!

49. Rosebud.

50. Romeo, Romeo wherefore art thou Romeo?

51. Random Fact.

52. Party time!

53. Party on, Wayne.

54. Open the pod bay doors.

55. One fish, two fish.

56. Never gonna give you up.

57. My name is Inigo Montoya.

58. More cowbell.

59. May the force be with you.

60. Make me a sandwich.

61. Make me [breakfast/dinner].

62. Mac or PC?

63. Live long and prosper.

64. Knock knock.

65. Is there a Santa?

66. Is the cake a lie?

67. Inconceivable.

68. I've seen things you people wouldn't believe.

69. I've fallen and I can't get up.

70. I'm home.

71. I want the truth!

72. I think you're funny.

73. I am your father.

74. I [love/hate] you.

75. How tall are you?

76. How much wood can a woodchuck chuck if a woodchuck could chuck wood?

77. How Much Wood can a Wood Chuck Chuck, if A Wood Chuck Could Chuck Norris

78. How much is that doggie in the window?

79. How much do you weigh?

80. How many pickled peppers did Peter Piper pick?

81. How many licks does it take to get to the center of a tootsie pop?

82. How many calories are in (name of food)?

83. How many angels can dance on the head of a pin?

84. How far is (location) from here?

85. How do you make bread?

86. How do I get rid of a dead body?

87. High five!

88. Good night.

89. Give me a hug.

90. Fire photon torpedoes.

91. Elementary, my dear Watson.

92. Does this unit have a soul?

93. Do you want to play a game?

94. Do you want to play a game?

95. Do you want to fight?

96. Do you want to build a snowman?

97. Do you really want to hurt me?

98. Do you like green eggs and ham?

99. Do you know the way to San Jose?

100.   Do you know the muffin man?

101.   Do you know Siri?

102.   Do you have any brothers or sisters?

103.   Do you have a girlfriend?

104.   Do you have a boyfriend?

105.   Do you believe in life after love?

106.   Do you believe in god?

107.   Do you believe in ghosts?

108.   Define supercalifragilisticexpialodocious.

109.   Count by ten.

110.   Can you give me some money? (ask twice)

111.   Beam me up.

Calculating Dates

Alexa has not yet learned to check how many days there are before the next Superbowl, but you can ask her the number of days before Christmas arrives. You can even ask her how many days are left until your birthday (any date, as long as you specify it) and Alexa will respond accordingly.

Hooking Up

No, it's not that you're going to date Alexa. It's more of connecting devices with the help of this web app called IFTTT, which stands for *If This Then That*.

If you have ever heard of IFTT, you will be very happy to know that they have made a channel for the Echo. IFTT (If This, Then That) is a web-based application that seeks to connect different "channels", triggering the action of another when a condition is met. This can greatly increase your productivity, and can ease your life overall. Currently, Alexa can talk to WeMo, Phillips Hue, and Wink, as well as the in-house Echo shopping and to do lists.

Some of the best IFTTT "recipes" include:

1. *I'd like to [call_____] 4PM today.*

You know how speed dials worked back in the day, right? Well, you can get a push notification to remind you that you need to call someone, and Alexa will tell you about it.

To create this recipe, choose *Launch Central* as your trigger center.

2. *[name] your message*

Email someone using Gmail, which is known as one of the most professional-looking email services around. Simply connect it to IFTTT and Alexa, and you're set.

3. *[feed my fish]*

If you have some fish to take care of, and you need to be reminded that they have to be fed already, you can ask the help of *LittleBits* and Alexa.

LittleBits is basically an open source library of electronic modules that you can use for learning and prototyping. It's like the cloud, but definitely safer, and more powerful.

4. *[today] your message*

Hey, it's still great not to let the art of journaling go to waste, you know? Sometimes, you may have some ideas in mind that you need to jot down right away, and you'd feel like having no pens or papers around you might be a problem—don't let it. What you can do is tell Alexa your message for it to directly be saved to *Google Drive.*

5. *[water the garden]*

There's a smart sprinkler controller called Iro, which can help you maintain your watering schedule, especially when you're so busy and you don't have much time for it. What's great about it is that it automatically changes and adjusts based on the season, and on the current state of the weather. This way, you'd only be using the right amount of water to make sure your garden/landscape is in good shape.

For this, you have to choose *Rancho Iro* as your trigger.

Playing Games

Of course, you could also play games with Alexa—she's pretty smart that way! For this, you could make use of the following commands:

1. *Alexa, heads or tails.* (She'll then say that she flipped a coin, and wil tell you whether she got head or tail!)

2. *Alexa, play Rock, Paper, Scissors.* (Alexa will answer with "*Alright, Let's play. 3, 2, 1, Rock/Paper/Scissors*". She can also play *Rock, Paper, Scissors, Lizard, Spock*—just like that game in *Big Bang Theory!*)

3. *Alexa, random number* (Alexa will give you a random number)

4. *Alexa, random number between x and y/Alexa, random number between 1 and 15, etc.* (Alexa will then give you a random number between x and y)

5. *Alexa, roll a die. (*She'll say that she has rolled the die and will give you a number between 1 to 6)

6. *Alexa, roll a N-sided die.* (She'll say that she has rolled a N-sided die and give you a number between 1 to N)

Connect Prime Accounts to Echo

This is actually easy. What you have to do is go to the settings page at www.echo.amazon.com, then choose Set up Household. Of course, it's imperative that members of your family also have Prime Accounts, too.

Now, your family members would just have to download the Echo App, and voila! He can now access Alexa, too!

Connect with Alexa on your computer

Aside from being able to control Alexa from its Android or iOS app, you can also just visit echo.amazon.com, and you'll be able to access to-do and shopping lists connected to Alexa.

Make Alexa say what she just said again

Just like when talking with other people, there may be times when you would not easily understand what Alexa has just said. What you can do then is ask Alexa to repeat her answer, and you can do this by saying *"Alexa, can you repeat that?"*. Make sure you say this calmly, because saying "Repeat that" without "Please" or "Can You" just makes Alexa a bit more stubborn, as she wouldn't really repeat it.

Use another account to access Alexa

Another great thing about Alexa is that you can actually control it even by using another Amazon account—as long as you have access to that account, of course. What you can do is ask Alexa which profile you're using. Now, make sure that this other Amazon Account of yours is connected to your original account. Ask Alexa to "switch profiles" (i.e., *Alexa, switch to Mary's Profile*) and you're all set!

Create a software update yourself

Just like all devices, software updates also happen to Alexa. But, the thing is, sometimes it feels like you have to wait for the updates and they come when you really do not want them to be there.

According to most users, software updates happen almost every night for Alexa, but if you don't want to wait for that time, go ahead, push the mute button, and allow Alexa to not do anything for at least 30 minutes. Updates would already happen then.

Make Alexa a bit stubborn

Of course, Alexa is named "Alexa". That is her Wake Word, which means that whenever you say "Alexa", she will respond. But, what if you're actually just talking about Alexa with your friends and you really don't want it to do anything?

Well, you can still make Alexa keep quiet. What you have to do is press the mute button on top of the device. After doing so, a red ring will be highlighted and Alexa would stay quiet until such time that you press the button again. This is important at times when you are just talking with your friends, or are in a meeting.

Chapter 8: Reminders and Warnings

Here are some of the things you have to keep in mind in order to make sure that the way you use Alexa will always be manageable and smooth-sailing:

Personalize It

Of course, you could customize Alexa to your liking!

To do this, launch the Echo app, go to *Settings > Device Location* then type the ZIP code where the Echo is located the tap *Save Changes*. This allows the Echo to know where you are and give you updated weather reports in your area everytime you ask. Next, change the metric measurements. Go to Settings then change the metrics used for distances, temperature, and measurements.

Making Use of Other Features and Making It Work in US Territories, Canada, and Mexico

In order to use other special features of Alexa, you have to make sure that you go to your app and then tap *Settings > Voice Purchasing*. Switch it on and then provide a confirmation code. This is a code that you have to create like as if you are creating a password. This code will be asked of you everytime you tell Alexa to make a purchase. Key in this 4-digit PIN and tap Save Changes.

Using the 1-Click Feature

The 1-Click feature is not a new concept. This has been with Amazon for years. If you are making regular purchase in Amazon, you know that the 1-Click feature is enabled when you provided your shipping address and billing information to Amazon. This allows you to click BUY online without ahv9ing to enter these details again. If you set this up on Echo, Alexa will simply get the information logged in your Amazon Account to complete the purchase.

Deleting Voice Recordings

In order to delete voice recordings on Alexa, just open the Alexa app, check Settings, choose History, look for one of those commands that you have made, tap it, and then hit the Delete button.

However, if you want to delete all of the recordings that are associated with your Alexa account and all connected device, you can do so by visiting amazon.com/mycd. Go *to Settings > Manage Content and Devices,* and then select the applicable products.

Household Aboard

The Amazon Echo is not exclusive to only one person. You can invite other adults to be part of the set-up so they can also enjoy using the device. To set this up, tap *Settings > Household Profiles > Invite.* Make sure that the person you are adding is present while you are setting his up. They need to key in their own PIN and details for Alexa to recognize them.

PIN Warning

And of course, it's also important to keep in mind that in order to confirm purchases (if any), you do need to use a PIN. Make sure though that you don't use your credit card PIN so you won't be susceptible to hacking or phishing. Just think of something else that you can easily remember—but that others won't easily guess.

Chapter 9: Solving Alexa's Problems

And finally, you have to expect that it's not every day that Alexa would work to the best of its abilities. In these cases, you have to make sure that you get to troubleshoot the problems—and you get them easily solved so you could enjoy using the device again!

Device not working properly

When the orange light on your Echo does not change to white, that means it cannot access the Wi-Fi. To troubleshoot, start by trying to reconnect to the network -- access the Echo app, go to Settings and click on "Update Wi-Fi". Then, follow the alternate set up guide we have mentioned above. Also, make sure that the network itself is not down -- the modem or router may have to be restarted to restore connectivity. Try bringing the Echo closer to the router, or removing any obstructions if possible.

If this does not work, try unplugging the Echo from the power cord for 3 seconds, then plugging it back. While doing this soft reset, check that your Echo has been properly registered in your Amazon account (this can be accessed online, under the "Manage Your Content and Devices" on the "Your Account" dropdown). This section of your Amazon account should correctly register your Echo's name. If all else fails, click "Deregister" under your Echo's name and go through the alternate set up process once again.

It doesn't connect to the cloud

Check the ring color. If the ring is circling blue or solid blue, it is active and connecting to the Amazon Cloud. You can go to *Settings > Echo > Sounds* to make Alexa produce a beeping sound whenever it is streaming to the cloud. Alexa will also produce an *end sound* once it is done searching. If nothing came up, then it means the search failed and you need to do it again.

It cannot understand what you are trying to say

Though Amazon has poured its engineering genius into the Echo's voice recognition system, there are times when it cannot understand your command clearly. The first step to resolving this is working on the Voice Training, which will be discussed in the next chapter. When doing the training, make sure that there is no background noise so Alexa can capture the words clearly.

When giving Alexa commands, as well, try minimizing the background noise. Speak clearly and slowly. It is also possible that the question is phrased improperly so Alexa cannot properly understand it.

If Alexa starts playing the wrong song for you, try checking on the app to see if she had understood the command properly. If she did, and the wrong song is still played, this could mean that the song you are asking for does not appear in your library.

If it is a question that Alexa cannot answer appropriately, try prefixing the word "question" before asking. Something like: "Alexa, question, <insert query here>?". Remember that Alexa is still learning, and does not know the answer to everything. Finally, if your question is something that Alexa needs to search the Web for (which is nearly all questions), make sure your WiFi network is properly connected.

It cannot connect to the remote

Troubleshooting an unpaired remote is much like the setup we have discussed earlier. First, make sure that the batteries are still working, then go through the set up process. If your device responds with a spinning purple light, this means that more than one remote is being detected. Hit the Play/Pause button on the one you wish to connect. Remember that only one remote can connect to the Echo at once.

It cannot connect to the Bluetooth

Like any other modern speaker worth its name, the Echo can interface with discovered Bluetooth devices. Remember that Bluetooth is a pretty limited connection and the paired devices will have to stay within 30 feet of each other.

When you speak the pair command to the Echo (i.e., "Alexa, pair to my phone"), check your Echo app to see if your phone has been found. Click "Connect" to pair. On the device being connected, make sure that Amazon Echo is selected for pairing.

If you still cannot connect, go to the app's settings and go to the "Bluetooth" option. Clear all currently paired devices by hitting "Remove", and attempt the pairing process once again. In the worst case, try resetting the device again by unplugging it from the power outlet for three seconds.

Resetting Alexa

If the basic troubleshooting steps here do not resolve the concern, you can do a complete factory reset of the Echo. Keep in mind that this will erase all settings, accounts, paired devices, etc. that you already entered -- essentially, it will be as if you have just unboxed the Echo.

To do this, get a paper clip or anything similar and look for the Reset button. This button is hidden deep within an unsuspecting hole in a notch near the power adapter port (at the bottom of the device). Press and hold this button, and the Light Ring will turn orange for a moment, and then blue. Wait for the ring to turn off then back on, and go through the entire setup process again.

Sending Feedback to Amazon

You can provide feedback by going to your app and selecting *Settings> Dialog History > Feedback > Send Email*. You can type your feedback here and send to Amazon.

Conclusion

I'd like to thank you and congratulate you for transiting my lines from start to finish.

I hope this book was able to help you to understand how to use Amazon Echo.

The next step is to keep the tips that you have read in this book in mind—and make sure that you apply them whenever you'd use the Echo. This way, you can be sure that you're able to maximize its use, and to make sure that it will really help you out.

I wish you the best of luck!

To your success,

Patrick Fisher

Made in the USA
Middletown, DE
09 June 2016